Mr. Sagar salunke has 10 years of experience in testing and JUnit. He has worked on large software testing projects in Software Companies in India, USA, UK, Australia and Switzerland.

His hobbies include travelling to new tourist places, watching basketball, cricket and learning latest technological stuff.

Preface

This book is for those who are new to Junit. It will help you understand what is Junit and how you can use it in your testing project.

Below topics are covered in this book.

1. Introduction to Junit
2. JUnit Set up - Integration with IDEs and Build tools like Maven, Gradle
3. JUnit Architecture
4. JUnit Annotations
5. JUnit Fixtures
6. Junit Assertions
7. Junit Categories
8. @Test Annotation Parameters
9. Verification of Exceptions
10. Ignoring tests
11. Time out in JUnit tests
12. Parameterizing tests
13. Test Suite
14. Rules in JUnit -
    TestWatcher, TemporaryFolder, ExternalResource
15. Theories in JUnit
16. JUnit Test Runners
17. Execution order of JUnit tests
18. Assumptions in JUnit
19. JUnit and Hamcrest Matchers

Table of Contents

1. Introduction to Junit

Junit is the most popular unit testing frameworks in Java world.

Key features of JUnit framework are given below.

1. Popular unit testing framework
2. Based on Test Driven Development
3. provides test fixtures allowing us to execute code for initialization and clean up
4. Support in all major IDEs like Eclipse, Intellij IDEA etc
5. Integrates seamlessly with build tools like Maven and Gradle
6. Tests can be categorized and run in groups
7. Tests can be ignored, timed and ordered to execute

2. JUnit Set up and installation

To start using JUnit, you will need below tools.

1. JDK
2. Intellij IDEA
3. Build tools like Maven or Gradle
4. JUnit dependency

Junit plug-ins are available for popular IDEs like Eclipse and Intellij IDEA. In Intellij IDEA, the JUnit plug-in is installed by default.

To add JUnit dependency in maven project, you need to add below xml block in POM.xml file.

```xml
<dependency>

    <groupId>junit</groupId>

    <artifactId>junit</artifactId>

    <version>4.11</version>

    <scope>test</scope>

</dependency>
```

To add JUnit dependency in Gradle project, you need to add below lines in build.gradle file.

```
dependencies
 {
    testCompile group: 'junit', name: 'junit',
version: '4.11'
 }
```

3. JUnit Architecture

JUnit architecture is very simple. You provide the list of test classes (and methods in it) to JUnit core. Then JUnit core reads each class, finds the test methods annotated with @Test and executes the tests one by one.

You can run tests in single class, multiple classes, all classes in package or directory. You can also run tests by category as well.

4. JUnit Annotations

Here is the list of annotations used in JUnit.

1. Fixture related - @Test, @Before, @After, @BeforeClass, @AfterClass
2. To ignore tests - @Ignore
3. Parameterized tests annotations - @RunWith(Parameterized.class), @Parameters
4. Suite related - @Suite.SuiteClasses, @RunWith(Suite.class)
5. Category related - @Category, @IncludeCategory, @ExcludeCategory
6. Rules related - @Rule
7. Theory and Assumptions related - @Theory, @DataPoint, @DataPoints, @FromDataPoints, @RunWith(Theories.class)

4.1 Basic Annotations in Junit

In this topic, you will learn about basic annotations in JUnit.

Here is the list of frequently used annotations in JUnit. Remember that all below annotations are put in org.junit package from JUnit 4.0 onwards

1. @Test - marks the method as test method
2. @BeforeClass - Method marked with this annotation is called once before all tests are run in particular class.
3. @AfterClass - Method marked with this annotation is called once afterall tests are run in particular class.
4. @Before - Method marked with this annotation is called once before each test is executed.
5. @After- Method marked with this annotation is called once after each test is executed.

```java
package junit_tests;

import org.junit.*;

/**
 * Created by Sagar on 28-03-2016.
 */

public class TestClass
{

    @BeforeClass
    public static void initialize()
    {
        //This method will be called once before all
tests are run in this class
        //do stuff here which you want to do only
once for all test methods
        //in this class like setting up environment,
allocating resources
        System.out.println("Before Class method");
    }

    @Before
    public void initMethod()
```

```java
    {
        //This method will be called once before
each test is run
        //In this method, do stuff which you want to
do before each test
        System.out.println("Before each test");
    }

    @Test
    public void test1()
    {
        System.out.println("Running test1");
        Assert.assertTrue("Checking simple
condition",1==1);

    }

    @Test
    public void test2()
    {
        System.out.println("Running test2");
        Assert.assertTrue("Checking other
condition",1==2);
    }

    @After
    public void cleanUpMethod()
    {
        //This method will be called once after each
test is run
        //In this method, do stuff which you want to
do after each test
        System.out.println("After each test");
    }

    @AfterClass
    public static void cleanUp()
    {
        //This method will be called once after all
tests are run in this class
        //do stuff here which you want to do only
once for all test methods
        //in this class like cleaning environment,
releasing resources
```

```
        System.out.println("After Class method");
    }
}
```

Here is the output of the above code.

junit_tests.MyTestRunner

Before Class method

Before each test

Running test1

After each test

Before each test

Running test2

After each test

After Class method

Total tests Ran 2

Total tests passed 1

Total tests failed 1

********Failed Tests*******

java.lang.AssertionError: Checking other condition

at org.junit.Assert.fail(Assert.java:88)

at org.junit.Assert.assertTrue(Assert.java:41)

at junit_tests.TestClass.test2(TestClass.java:35)

at sun.reflect.NativeMethodAccessorImpl.invoke0(Native Method)

at sun.reflect.NativeMethodAccessorImpl.invoke(NativeMethodAccessorImpl.java:62)

at sun.reflect.DelegatingMethodAccessorImpl.invoke(DelegatingMethodAccessorImpl.java:43) at java.lang.reflect.Method.invoke(Method.java:498)

at

org.junit.runners.model.FrameworkMethod$1.runReflecti
veCall(FrameworkMethod.java:47)

at

org.junit.internal.runners.model.ReflectiveCallable.run(Ref
lectiveCallable.java:12)

at

org.junit.runners.model.FrameworkMethod.invokeExplosi
vely(FrameworkMethod.java:44)

at

org.junit.internal.runners.statements.InvokeMethod.evalu
ate(InvokeMethod.java:17)

at

org.junit.internal.runners.statements.RunBefores.evaluate
(RunBefores.java:26)

at

org.junit.internal.runners.statements.RunAfters.evaluate(
RunAfters.java:27)

at

org.junit.runners.ParentRunner.runLeaf(ParentRunner.jav
a:271)

at

org.junit.runners.BlockJUnit4ClassRunner.runChild(BlockJU
nit4ClassRunner.java:70)

at

org.junit.runners.BlockJUnit4ClassRunner.runChild(BlockJU
nit4ClassRunner.java:50)

at

org.junit.runners.ParentRunner$3.run(ParentRunner.java:
238)

at
org.junit.runners.ParentRunner$1.schedule(ParentRunner.
java:63)
at
org.junit.runners.ParentRunner.runChildren(ParentRunner
.java:236)
at
org.junit.runners.ParentRunner.access$000(ParentRunner.
java:53)
at
org.junit.runners.ParentRunner$2.evaluate(ParentRunner.
java:229)
at
org.junit.internal.runners.statements.RunBefores.evaluate
(RunBefores.java:26)
at
org.junit.internal.runners.statements.RunAfters.evaluate(
RunAfters.java:27)
at
org.junit.runners.ParentRunner.run(ParentRunner.java:30
9)
at org.junit.runners.Suite.runChild(Suite.java:127)
at org.junit.runners.Suite.runChild(Suite.java:26)
at
org.junit.runners.ParentRunner$3.run(ParentRunner.java:
238)
at
org.junit.runners.ParentRunner$1.schedule(ParentRunner.
java:63)
at
org.junit.runners.ParentRunner.runChildren(ParentRunner

.java:236)

at

org.junit.runners.ParentRunner.access$000(ParentRunner.java:53)

at

org.junit.runners.ParentRunner$2.evaluate(ParentRunner.java:229)

at

org.junit.runners.ParentRunner.run(ParentRunner.java:309)

at org.junit.runner.JUnitCore.run(JUnitCore.java:160)

at org.junit.runner.JUnitCore.run(JUnitCore.java:138)

at org.junit.runner.JUnitCore.run(JUnitCore.java:128)

at

org.junit.runner.JUnitCore.runClasses(JUnitCore.java:73)

at junit_tests.MyTestRunner.main(MyTestRunner.java:13)

at sun.reflect.NativeMethodAccessorImpl.invoke0(Native Method)

at

sun.reflect.NativeMethodAccessorImpl.invoke(NativeMethodAccessorImpl.java:62)

at

sun.reflect.DelegatingMethodAccessorImpl.invoke(DelegatingMethodAccessorImpl.java:43)

at java.lang.reflect.Method.invoke(Method.java:498)

at

com.intellij.rt.execution.application.AppMain.main(AppMain.java:144)

********Test were successful*******
false

Process finished with exit code 0

4.2 How to ignore JUnit tests

Sometimes you want to skip some tests. SO JUnit provides annotation called as @Ignore which helps us to ignore tests.

Below example will illustrate how to use @Ignore annotation.

```java
import org.junit.*;
import static org.junit.Assert.assertTrue;

/**
 * Created by Sagar on 28-03-2016.
 */
public class IgnoreTestClass
{

    @Test @Ignore
    public void test1()
    {
        System.out.println("**Running test from
sanity**");
        assertTrue("Checking simple
condition",1==1);
    }

    @Test
    public void test2()
    {
        System.out.println("Running test2");
        Assert.assertEquals("Checking other
condition","sagar","sagar");
    }
}
```

After running above JUnit class only second test will be executed as first test method is annotated with @Ignore.

We can also ignore entire test class by annotating the class by @Ignore as shown in below example.

```java
package junit_tests;

import org.junit.*;
import static org.junit.Assert.assertTrue;

/**
 * Created by Sagar on 28-03-2016.
 */
@Ignore
public class IgnoreTestClass
{

    @Test
    public void test1()
    {
        System.out.println("**Running test from sanity**");
        assertTrue("Checking simple condition",1==1);
    }

    @Test
    public void test2()
    {
        System.out.println("Running test2");
        Assert.assertEquals("Checking other condition","sagar","sagar");
    }
}
```

4.3 Parameterized tests in Junit

Sometimes we need to follow same steps to test something. But the input is different. In that case, you do not need to create a separate test method for each input. That's when parameterized tests come into picture.

Below example will illustrate how to use parameterized tests. Test method testOddEven will run 5 times each for 5 input numbers.

```java
package junit_tests;

import java.util.Arrays;
import java.util.Collection;

import org.junit.Test;
import org.junit.runners.Parameterized;
import org.junit.runner.RunWith;
import static org.junit.Assert.assertTrue;

@RunWith(Parameterized.class)
public class JunitParametersClass
{
    private Integer number;
    private String expectedResult;

    public JunitParametersClass(Integer number,
                                String
expectedResult)
    {
        this.number = number;
        this.expectedResult = expectedResult;
    }

    @Parameterized.Parameters
    public static Collection Numbers()
    {
        return Arrays.asList(new Object[][]
```

```
        {
                { 1, "odd" },
                { 2, "even" },
                { 3, "odd"},
                { 4, "even" },
                { 5, "odd"}
        });
    }

    @Test
    public void testOddEven()
    {
        System.out.println("Number is : " + number);
        if (expectedResult.equalsIgnoreCase("odd"))
            assertTrue(number %2!=0);
        else
            assertTrue(number %2==0);
    }
}
```

4.4 Running multiple test classes using JUnit suite

JUnit allows you to run all tests in specific test classes by using a concept called as JUnit suite.

Below example illustrates how to Suite.class to run the test methods in given classes. In below example, We have asked JUnit to run the tests from TestClass.class and IgnoreTestClass.class. We can pass the list of any number of classes to run the tests from.

```
package junit_tests;

import org.junit.runner.RunWith;
import org.junit.runners.Suite;
@RunWith(Suite.class)
```

```
@Suite.SuiteClasses({
        TestClass.class,
        IgnoreTestClass.class
})
public class JunitSuiteClass
{
}
```

4.5 JUnit categories

When we ask JUnit to run the tests in specific class, all tests are executed in that class. What if want to run specific tests?

That's when JUnit categories come in to picture. With JUnit categories we can tag tests to specific category and then execute tests from that specific categories.

Maven and Gradle also allows us to configure the JUnit to run tests from specific categories.

Let say you want to run the tests with category SanityTests, then create an interface with name SanityTests.

```
public interface SanityTests { }
```

After that create test class as shown in below example. Note how we have tagged a method to be of category - SanityTests

```
package junit_tests;

import static org.junit.Assert.*;

import junit_categories.SanityTests;
```

```java
import org.junit.*;
import org.junit.experimental.categories.Category;
/**
* Created by Sagar on 28-03-2016.
*/
public class TestClass
{

@BeforeClass
public static void initialize()
{
//This method will be called once before all tests
are run in this class
//do stuff here which you want to do only once for
all test methods
//in this class like setting up environment,
allocating resources
System.out.println("Before Class method");
}

@Before
public void initMethod()
{
//This method will be called once before each test
is run
//In this method, do stuff which you want to do
before each test
System.out.println("Before each test");
}

@Category(SanityTests.class)
@Test
public void test1()
{
System.out.println("**Running test from sanity**");
assertTrue("Checking simple condition",1==1);
}

@Test
public void test2()
{
System.out.println("Running test2");
Assert.assertTrue("Checking other condition",1==2);
}
```

```
@After
public void cleanUpMethod()
{
//This method will be called once after each test is
run
//In this method, do stuff which you want to do
after each test
System.out.println("After each test");
}

@AfterClass
public static void cleanUp()
{
//This method will be called once after all tests
are run in this class
//do stuff here which you want to do only once for
all test methods
//in this class like cleaning environment, releasing
resources
System.out.println("After Class method");
}
}
```

After that create a class as shown in below example. Note that we are using @RunWith annotation which tells JUnit that we are trying to execute the tests of specific category.

```
package junit_tests;

import junit_categories.SanityTests;
import org.junit.experimental.categories.Categories;
import org.junit.runner.RunWith;
import org.junit.runners.Suite;

@RunWith(Categories.class)
@Categories.IncludeCategory(SanityTests.class)
@Suite.SuiteClasses( {TestClass.class})
public class CategoryTests
{
```

```
}
```

4.6 JUnit Theories

Junit Theories allow you to test theories with all possible combinations of data points.

For example - Consider below mathematical expression.

a+b > a and a+b > b where a,b > 0

Above expressions are always true for all combination of values of a and b.

To test above theory, we can write a simple test and verify it. But To test above expressions with many data points, we will have to write more code. But JUnit theories can test many data points very easily.

Below example explains how we can use Theories in JUnit to verify below theories.

1. $(a+b)^2 = a^2 + b^2 + 2*a*b$
2. a+b > a, a+b > b where a, b > 0

```
package theories;

import org.junit.Assume;
import org.junit.experimental.theories.DataPoints;
import org.junit.experimental.theories.Theories;
import org.junit.experimental.theories.Theory;
import org.junit.runner.RunWith;
import static org.junit.Assert.assertEquals;
import static org.junit.Assert.assertTrue;
```

```java
@RunWith(Theories.class)
public class MyJunitTheories
{

    @DataPoints
    public static int[] dataPoints()
    {
        return new int[]
        {
                71, 82, 53,-1
        };
    }


    //For a and b where a,b > 0
    //(a+b)^2 = a^2+b^2+2ab
    //a+b > a and a+b > b
    @Theory
    public void squareTheory(Integer a, Integer b)
    {
        //Below assume statement ensures that we are
testing only positive numbers
        Assume.assumeTrue(a > 0 && b > 0);

        System.out.println("Running with Data points
- " + a + " , "+ b);

        Double leftSide = Math.pow(a+b,2);
        Double rightSide = Double.valueOf(a * a + b
* b + 2 * a * b);

        assertEquals(leftSide,rightSide);
        assertTrue(a + b > a);
        assertTrue(a + b > b);
    }

}
```

Here is the output of above code.

Running with Data points - 71 , 71

Running with Data points - 71 , 82

Running with Data points - 71 , 53
Running with Data points - 82 , 71
Running with Data points - 82 , 82
Running with Data points - 82 , 53
Running with Data points - 53 , 71
Running with Data points - 53 , 82
Running with Data points - 53 , 53

5. Basic Annotations in Junit

In this topic, you will learn about basic annotations in JUnit.

Here is the list of frequently used annotations in JUnit. Remember that all below annotations are put in org.junit package from JUnit 4.0 onwards

1. @Test - marks the method as test method
2. @BeforeClass - Method marked with this annotation is called once before all tests are run in particular class.
3. @AfterClass - Method marked with this annotation is called once afterall tests are run in particular class.
4. @Before - Method marked with this annotation is called once before each test is executed.
5. @After- Method marked with this annotation is called once after each test is executed.

```
package junit_tests;

import org.junit.*;

/**
 * Created by Sagar on 28-03-2016.
 */
public class TestClass
{

    @BeforeClass
    public static void initialize()
```

```
    {
        //This method will be called once before all
tests are run in this class
        //do stuff here which you want to do only
once for all test methods
        //in this class like setting up environment,
allocating resources
        System.out.println("Before Class method");
    }

    @Before
    public void initMethod()
    {
        //This method will be called once before
each test is run
        //In this method, do stuff which you want to
do before each test
        System.out.println("Before each test");
    }

    @Test
    public void test1()
    {
        System.out.println("Running test1");
        Assert.assertTrue("Checking simple
condition",1==1);

    }

    @Test
    public void test2()
    {
        System.out.println("Running test2");
        Assert.assertTrue("Checking other
condition",1==2);
    }

    @After
    public void cleanUpMethod()
    {
        //This method will be called once after each
test is run
        //In this method, do stuff which you want to
do after each test
```

```
            System.out.println("After each test");
    }

    @AfterClass
    public static void cleanUp()
    {
        //This method will be called once after all
tests are run in this class
        //do stuff here which you want to do only
once for all test methods
        //in this class like cleaning environment,
releasing resources
        System.out.println("After Class method");
    }
}
```

Here is the output of the above code.

junit_tests.MyTestRunner

Before Class method

Before each test

Running test1

After each test

Before each test

Running test2

After each test

After Class method

Total tests Ran 2

Total tests passed 1

Total tests failed 1

********Failed Tests*******

java.lang.AssertionError: Checking other condition

at org.junit.Assert.fail(Assert.java:88)

at org.junit.Assert.assertTrue(Assert.java:41)

at junit_tests.TestClass.test2(TestClass.java:35)

at sun.reflect.NativeMethodAccessorImpl.invoke0(Native Method)

at sun.reflect.NativeMethodAccessorImpl.invoke(NativeMethodAccessorImpl.java:62)

at sun.reflect.DelegatingMethodAccessorImpl.invoke(DelegatingMethodAccessorImpl.java:43)

at java.lang.reflect.Method.invoke(Method.java:498)

at org.junit.runners.model.FrameworkMethod$1.runReflectiveCall(FrameworkMethod.java:47)

at org.junit.internal.runners.model.ReflectiveCallable.run(ReflectiveCallable.java:12)

at org.junit.runners.model.FrameworkMethod.invokeExplosively(FrameworkMethod.java:44)

at org.junit.internal.runners.statements.InvokeMethod.evaluate(InvokeMethod.java:17)

at org.junit.internal.runners.statements.RunBefores.evaluate(RunBefores.java:26)

at org.junit.internal.runners.statements.RunAfters.evaluate(RunAfters.java:27)

at org.junit.runners.ParentRunner.runLeaf(ParentRunner.java:271)

at
org.junit.runners.BlockJUnit4ClassRunner.runChild(BlockJU
nit4ClassRunner.java:70)

at
org.junit.runners.BlockJUnit4ClassRunner.runChild(BlockJU
nit4ClassRunner.java:50)

at
org.junit.runners.ParentRunner$3.run(ParentRunner.java:
238)

at
org.junit.runners.ParentRunner$1.schedule(ParentRunner.
java:63)

at
org.junit.runners.ParentRunner.runChildren(ParentRunner
.java:236)

at
org.junit.runners.ParentRunner.access$000(ParentRunner.
java:53)

at
org.junit.runners.ParentRunner$2.evaluate(ParentRunner.
java:229)

at
org.junit.internal.runners.statements.RunBefores.evaluate
(RunBefores.java:26)

at
org.junit.internal.runners.statements.RunAfters.evaluate(
RunAfters.java:27)

at
org.junit.runners.ParentRunner.run(ParentRunner.java:30
9)

at org.junit.runners.Suite.runChild(Suite.java:127)

at org.junit.runners.Suite.runChild(Suite.java:26)

at
org.junit.runners.ParentRunner$3.run(ParentRunner.java:
238)

at
org.junit.runners.ParentRunner$1.schedule(ParentRunner.
java:63)

at
org.junit.runners.ParentRunner.runChildren(ParentRunner
.java:236)

at
org.junit.runners.ParentRunner.access$000(ParentRunner.
java:53)

at
org.junit.runners.ParentRunner$2.evaluate(ParentRunner.
java:229)

at
org.junit.runners.ParentRunner.run(ParentRunner.java:30
9)

at org.junit.runner.JUnitCore.run(JUnitCore.java:160)
at org.junit.runner.JUnitCore.run(JUnitCore.java:138)
at org.junit.runner.JUnitCore.run(JUnitCore.java:128)

at
org.junit.runner.JUnitCore.runClasses(JUnitCore.java:73)
at junit_tests.MyTestRunner.main(MyTestRunner.java:13)
at sun.reflect.NativeMethodAccessorImpl.invoke0(Native
Method)

at
sun.reflect.NativeMethodAccessorImpl.invoke(NativeMeth
odAccessorImpl.java:62)

at

sun.reflect.DelegatingMethodAccessorImpl.invoke(Delegat
ingMethodAccessorImpl.java:43)

at java.lang.reflect.Method.invoke(Method.java:498)

at
com.intellij.rt.execution.application.AppMain.main(AppMa
in.java:144)

********Test were successful*******

false

Process finished with exit code 0

6. Junit Assertions

Assertions are used to decide if the test passes or fails. If the assertion is successful, test will pass. Otherwise it will fail.

org.junit.Assert class provides various methods that can be used to do assertions in tests. There are various types of assertions in JUnit.

1. assertTrue and assertFalse - checks if expression returns true or false.
2. assertArrayEquals - checks if 2 arrays have equals values.
3. assertEquals - checks if 2 objects are equal.
4. assertNull and assertNotNull - checks if expression is null or not null.
5. assertSame and assertNotSame - checks if the 2 objects refer to same object.
6. assertThat - Asserts that actual satisfies the condition specified by matcher.

All above methods have various signatures. For example - assertTrue method has 2 signatures as mentioned below. In first method, we can pass the message which we want to print in the console output which can be used for troubleshooting.

1. assertTrue(String x, boolean y)
2. assertTrue(boolean y)

Similarly we have different signatures for all other methods.

Here is an example which shows how to use assertTrue and assertEquals

```
@Test
    public void test1()
    {
        System.out.println("Running test1");
        assertTrue("Checking simple
condition",1==1);
        assertEquals("Assert if strings are same",
"softpost.org","softpost.com");
    }
```

Here is the output of above code.

Before Class methodBefore each test

Running test1

After each test

org.junit.ComparisonFailure: Assert if strings are same

Expected :softpost.org

Actual   :softpost.com

<Click to see difference>

at org.junit.Assert.assertEquals(Assert.java:115)

at junit_tests.TestClass.test1(TestClass.java:31)

at
sun.reflect.NativeMethodAccessorImpl.invoke0(Native Method)

After Class method

Process finished with exit code -1

7. Junit Categories

When we ask JUnit to run the tests in specific class, all tests are executed in that class. What if want to run specific tests?

That's when JUnit categories come in to picture. With JUnit categories we can tag tests to specific category and then execute tests from that specific categories.

Maven and Gradle also allows us to configure the JUnit to run tests from specific categories.

Let say you want to run the tests with category SanityTests, then create an interface with name SanityTests.

```
public interface SanityTests { }
```

After that create test class as shown in below example. Note how we have tagged a method to be of category - SanityTests

```
package junit_tests;

import static org.junit.Assert.*;

import junit_categories.SanityTests;
import org.junit.*;
import org.junit.experimental.categories.Category;
/**
 * Created by Sagar on 28-03-2016.
 */
public class TestClass
{
```

```java
@BeforeClass
public static void initialize()
{
//This method will be called once before all tests
are run in this class
//do stuff here which you want to do only once for
all test methods
//in this class like setting up environment,
allocating resources
System.out.println("Before Class method");
}

@Before
public void initMethod()
{
//This method will be called once before each test
is run
//In this method, do stuff which you want to do
before each test
System.out.println("Before each test");
}

@Category(SanityTests.class)
@Test
public void test1()
{
System.out.println("**Running test from sanity**");
assertTrue("Checking simple condition",1==1);
}

@Test
public void test2()
{
System.out.println("Running test2");
Assert.assertTrue("Checking other condition",1==2);
}

@After
public void cleanUpMethod()
{
//This method will be called once after each test is
run
```

```
//In this method, do stuff which you want to do
after each test
System.out.println("After each test");
}

@AfterClass
public static void cleanUp()
{
//This method will be called once after all tests
are run in this class
//do stuff here which you want to do only once for
all test methods
//in this class like cleaning environment, releasing
resources
System.out.println("After Class method");
}
}
```

After that create a class as shown in below example. Note that we are using @RunWith annotation which tells JUnit that we are trying to execute the tests of specific category.

```
package junit_tests;

import junit_categories.SanityTests;
import org.junit.experimental.categories.Categories;
import org.junit.runner.RunWith;
import org.junit.runners.Suite;

@RunWith(Categories.class)
@Categories.IncludeCategory(SanityTests.class)
@Suite.SuiteClasses( {TestClass.class})
public class CategoryTests
{
}
```

8. @Test Annotation Parameters

Here is the list of parameters that can be passed to @Test Annotation in JUnit.

1. @Test(expected=IOException.class)
2. @Test(timeout=100)
3. @Test(dataProvider = "Wordpressdata")

expected parameter is used to verify that specific exception is thrown by the test.

timeout parameter is used to specify the timeout of the test. If the test takes more time than given timeout, test fails.

dataprovider is used to pass the test data to test from data source.

9. Verification of Exceptions

Generally whenever a test throws any exception, JUnit fails that test. But some times the exceptions are expected So test should pass when the exception occur.

Below example will illustrate how to test exceptions in JUnit tests. Note how we have used expected parameter in @Test annotation.

```java
@Test(expected = ArithmeticException.class)

public void testException()

{

   System.out.println("Running Exception test");

   int k = 0 ;

   int b = 100/k;

}
```

Above test will pass after execution as the Arithmetic exception is thrown in last line. So that's how we can check for any kind of exception in JUnit tests.

10. How to ignore JUnit tests

Sometimes you want to skip some tests. SO JUnit provides annotation called as @Ignore which helps us to ignore tests.

Below example will illustrate how to use @Ignore annotation.

```java
import org.junit.*;

import static org.junit.Assert.assertTrue;
/**
 * Created by Sagar on 28-03-2016.
 */

public class IgnoreTestClass

{

    @Test @Ignore

    public void test1()

    {

        System.out.println("**Running test from sanity**");

        assertTrue("Checking simple condition",1==1);

    }
```

```
    @Test

    public void test2()

    {

        System.out.println("Running test2");

        Assert.assertEquals("Checking other
condition","sagar","sagar");

    }

}
```

After running above JUnit class only second test will be executed as first test method is annotated with @Ignore.

We can also ignore entire test class by annotating the class by @Ignore as shown in below example.

```
package junit_tests;

import org.junit.*;
import static org.junit.Assert.assertTrue;

/**
 * Created by Sagar on 28-03-2016.
 */
@Ignore
public class IgnoreTestClass
{

    @Test
    public void test1()
    {
        System.out.println("**Running test from
sanity**");
```

```
        assertTrue("Checking simple
condition",1==1);
    }

    @Test
    public void test2()
    {
        System.out.println("Running test2");
        Assert.assertEquals("Checking other
condition","sagar","sagar");
    }
}
```

11. Time out in JUnit tests

Some tests take short time to run while others might take longer to run. Sometimes we have to fail the test if it is taking longer than specified amount of duration.

JUnit provides timeout parameter which can be used to fail the test if it takes longer than expected time to execute.

Below example will illustrate how we can use timeout parameter in JUnit tests. Below test will fail as it takes longer than 1 second to execute.

```java
package junit_tests;

import org.junit.Test;
import static org.junit.Assert.assertTrue;

public class TimeoutTestClass
{

    @Test(timeout=1000)
    public void test1() throws Exception
    {
        System.out.println("**Running test from
sanity**");
        Thread.sleep(5000);
        assertTrue("Checking simple
condition",1==1);
    }
}
```

Here is the output above test execution.

Running test from sanity

java.lang.Exception: test timed out after 1000 milliseconds

at java.lang.Thread.sleep(Native Method)

12. Parameterizing tests

Sometimes we need to follow same steps to test something. But the input is different. In that case, you do not need to create a separate test method for each input. That's when parameterized tests come into picture.

Below example will illustrate how to use parameterized tests. Test method testOddEven will run 5 times each for 5 input numbers.

```
package junit_tests;
import java.util.Arrays;
import java.util.Collection;

import org.junit.Test;
import org.junit.runners.Parameterized;
import org.junit.runner.RunWith;
import static org.junit.Assert.assertTrue;

@RunWith(Parameterized.class)
public class JunitParametersClass
{
    private Integer number;
    private String expectedResult;

    public JunitParametersClass(Integer number,
                                String
expectedResult)
    {
        this.number = number;
        this.expectedResult = expectedResult;
    }

    @Parameterized.Parameters
    public static Collection Numbers()
    {
        return Arrays.asList(new Object[][]
```

```
        {
                { 1, "odd" },
                { 2, "even" },
                { 3, "odd"},
                { 4, "even" },
                { 5, "odd"}
        });
    }

    @Test
    public void testOddEven()
    {
        System.out.println("Number is : " + number);
        if (expectedResult.equalsIgnoreCase("odd"))
            assertTrue(number %2!=0);
        else
            assertTrue(number %2==0);
    }
}
```

13. Test Suite

JUnit allows you to run all tests in specific test classes by using a concept called as JUnit suite.

Below example illustrates how to Suite.class to run the test methods in given classes. In below example, We have asked JUnit to run the tests from TestClass.class and IgnoreTestClass.class. We can pass the list of any number of classes to run the tests from.

```java
package junit_tests;

import org.junit.runner.RunWith;
import org.junit.runners.Suite;
@RunWith(Suite.class)
@Suite.SuiteClasses({
        TestClass.class,
        IgnoreTestClass.class
})
public class JunitSuiteClass
{
}
```

14. Rules in JUnit

14.1 TestWatcher rule in Junit

TestWatcher rule allows you to log the status of each test as it runs. Notice how we override below methods.

1. succeeded
2. finished
3. failed
4. skipped
5. starting

Below example explains how you can use TestWatcher rule in JUnit tests.

```java
package rules;

import org.junit.AssumptionViolatedException;
import org.junit.Ignore;
import org.junit.Rule;
import org.junit.Test;
import org.junit.rules.TestRule;
import org.junit.rules.TestWatcher;
import org.junit.runner.Description;
import org.junit.runners.model.Statement;

public class TestWatcherRule
{

    @Rule
    public TestRule testWatcher = new TestWatcher()
{
        @Override
        public Statement apply(Statement base,
Description description)
        {
```

```java
                return super.apply(base, description);
        }

        @Override
        protected void succeeded(Description
description)
        {
                System.out.println("Test " +
description.getDisplayName() + " passed");
        }

        @Override
        protected void failed(Throwable e,
Description description)
        {
                System.out.println("Test " +
description.getDisplayName() + " failed");
        }

        @Override
        protected void
skipped(AssumptionViolatedException e, Description
description)
        {
                System.out.println("Test " +
description.getDisplayName() + " skipped");
        }

        @Override
        protected void starting(Description
description)
        {
                super.starting(description);
                System.out.println("Test " +
description.getDisplayName() +" Started");
        }

        @Override
        protected void finished(Description
description)
        {
                super.finished(description);
                System.out.println("Test " +
description.getDisplayName() + " finished.");
```

```
        }
    };

    @Test
    public void simpleMathTest()
    {
        assert 5==3+2;
    }

    @Test
    public void complexMathTest()
    {
        assert Math.sqrt(625)==26;
    }

    @Test @Ignore
    public void stringTest()
    {
        assert "www.softpost.org".length() == 10;
    }
}
```

Here is the output of above code.

Test ignored.Test simpleMathTest(rules.TestWatcherRule)
Started

Test simpleMathTest(rules.TestWatcherRule) passed

Test simpleMathTest(rules.TestWatcherRule) finished.

Test complexMathTest(rules.TestWatcherRule) Started

Test complexMathTest(rules.TestWatcherRule) failed

Test complexMathTest(rules.TestWatcherRule) finished.

java.lang.AssertionError

14.2 Temporary folder rule in Junit

Temporary folder rule allows you to create a temporary folder every time you run the test.

Below example demonstrates how we can use temporary folder rule. Notice that in both tests, a new temporary folder is created.

```java
package rules;

import org.junit.Rule;
import org.junit.Test;
import org.junit.rules.TemporaryFolder;

import java.io.File;
import java.io.IOException;

public class TempFolderRule
{

    @Rule
    public TemporaryFolder tempFolder = new
TemporaryFolder();

    @Test
    public void testUsingTempFolder() throws
IOException
    {
        System.out.println("Creating a simple file
in a temp folder");
        File testFile =
tempFolder.newFile("testfile.txt");

System.out.println(testFile.getAbsolutePath());
        System.out.println("Creating a simple folder
in a temp folder");
        File testfolder =
tempFolder.newFolder("testfolder");
```

```
        System.out.println("Deleting temp folder..No
need to delete explicitly");
        tempFolder.delete();
    }

    @Test
    public void testAnotherTempFolder() throws
IOException
    {
        System.out.println("Creating a other file in
a temp folder");
        File testFile =
tempFolder.newFile("otherTestfile.txt");

System.out.println(testFile.getAbsolutePath());
    }
}
```

Here is the output of above example.

Creating a simple file in a temp folder
C:\Users\Sagar\AppData\Local\Temp\junit1357048258081
112491\testfile.txt
Creating a simple folder in a temp folder
Deleting temp folder..No need to delete explicitly
Creating a other file in a temp folder
C:\Users\Sagar\AppData\Local\Temp\junit3158376973255
21595\otherTestfile.txt

14.3 ExternalResource rule in Junit

ExternalResource rule allows you to use any resource in
your test without worrying about how to instantiate that
resource.

Below example explains how you can
use ExternalResource test rule in JUnit tests. Note that
how we have used before and after methods
of ExternalResource to initialize and destroy the external
resource respectively.

```java
package rules;

import org.junit.Rule;
import org.junit.Test;
import org.junit.rules.ExternalResource;

/**
 * Created by Sagar on 25-04-2016.
 */
public class ExternalResourceRuleTest
{

    Database cn = new Database();

    @Rule
    public ExternalResource resource = new
ExternalResource()
    {
        @Override
        protected void before() throws Throwable
        {
            cn.connect();
        };

        @Override
        protected void after()
        {
            cn.disconnect();
        };
    };

    @Test
    public void testDatabase()
    {
        cn.getData();
```

```
            System.out.println("code to test database
follows");
        }
}

class Database
{
    public void connect()
    {
        System.out.println("Connecting");
    }

    public void disconnect()
    {
        System.out.println("Dis-connecting");
    }

    public void getData()
    {
        System.out.println("Getting data");
    }
}
```

Here is the output of above code.

Connecting

Getting data

code to test database follows

Dis-connecting

15. JUnit Theories

Junit Theories allow you to test theories with all possible combinations of data points.

For example - Consider below mathematical expression.

a+b > a and a+b > b where a,b > 0

Above expressions are always true for all combination of values of a and b.

To test above theory, we can write a simple test and verify it. But To test above expressions with many data points, we will have to write more code. But JUnit theories can test many data points very easily.

Below example explains how we can use Theories in JUnit to verify below theories.

1. $(a+b)^2 = a^2 + b^2 + 2*a*b$
2. a+b > a, a+b > b where a, b > 0

```
package theories;

import org.junit.Assume;
import org.junit.experimental.theories.DataPoints;
import org.junit.experimental.theories.Theories;
import org.junit.experimental.theories.Theory;
import org.junit.runner.RunWith;
import static org.junit.Assert.assertEquals;
import static org.junit.Assert.assertTrue;

@RunWith(Theories.class)
public class MyJunitTheories
{
```

```
@DataPoints
public static int[] dataPoints()
{
    return new int[]
    {
            71, 82, 53,-1
    };
}

//For a and b where a,b > 0
//(a+b)^2 = a^2+b^2+2ab
//a+b > a and a+b > b
@Theory
public void squareTheory(Integer a, Integer b)
{
    //Below assume statement ensures that we are
testing only positive numbers
    Assume.assumeTrue(a > 0 && b > 0);

    System.out.println("Running with Data points
- " + a + " , "+ b);

    Double leftSide = Math.pow(a+b,2);
    Double rightSide = Double.valueOf(a * a + b
* b + 2 * a * b);

    assertEquals(leftSide,rightSide);
    assertTrue(a + b > a);
    assertTrue(a + b > b);
}

}
```

Here is the output of above code.

Running with Data points - 71 , 71

Running with Data points - 71 , 82

Running with Data points - 71 , 53

Running with Data points - 82 , 71

Running with Data points - 82 , 82
Running with Data points - 82 , 53
Running with Data points - 53 , 71
Running with Data points - 53 , 82
Running with Data points - 53 , 53

16. JUnit Test Runners

In this topic, let us learn about various test runners available to run JUnit tests.

Using IDE

All popular IDEs like Eclipse, IntelliJ IDEA, Net beans provide plug-ins to run JUnit tests from within IDE.

Using command line

We can also run the tests from command line using below syntax.

```
java org.junit.runner.JUnitCore MyTestClass1
MyTestClass2 MyTestClass3
```

Using runClasses method of JUnitCore class

We can also run JUnit tests using JUnitCore class. This class provides a method called as runClasses to which we can pass list of classes to be run. In below example, tests from 2 test classes will be run - OrderedTests and HamcrestTests.

```
package runners;

import hamcrest.TestHamcrest;
import ordered_tests.OrderedTests;
import org.junit.runner.JUnitCore;

/**
 * Created by Sagar on 30-04-2016.
 */
```

```java
public class JunitRunners
{

    public static void main(String [] args)
    {
        JUnitCore.runClasses(OrderedTests.class,
HamcrestTests.class);
    }
}
```

Using custom Runners

We can also have custom runners as well created using @RunWith annotation. For example, popular BDD framework cucumber uses custom runner to run JUnit tests using @RunWith annotation.

17. Execution order of JUnit tests

JUnit does not run the tests in the order they are written in a test class. So there is no guarantee of which tests will run in which order.

But sometimes it is important to run the tests in typical order. JUnit 4.12+ provides annotation called as @FixMethodOrder. We can pass one parameter to this annotation called as MethodSorters.NAME_ASCENDING

With this annotation parameter, tests are always run in ascending order of names of test methods. For example, in below test class, tests will always be run in below order.

1. abcTest()
2. pqrTest()
3. xyzTest()

Without @FixMethodOrder(MethodSorters.NAME_ASCEN DING), there is no guarantee of order in which tests are executed.

```
package ordered_tests;

import org.junit.FixMethodOrder;
import org.junit.Test;
import org.junit.runners.MethodSorters;

/**
 * Created by Sagar on 30-04-2016.
 */

    @FixMethodOrder(MethodSorters.NAME_ASCENDING)
    public class OrderedTests
```

```
{

    @Test
    public void abcTest()
    {
        System.out.println("ABC");
    }

    @Test
    public void pqrTest()
    {
        System.out.println("PQR");
    }

    @Test
    public void xyzTest()
    {
        System.out.println("XYZ");
    }

}
```

Here is the output of above test.

ABC
PQR
XYZ

18. Assumptions in JUnit

Assumptions in JUnit allow you to specify the condition which should be met before executing certain tests.

For example - some times it is important to ensure that service is running before executing the tests. If service is not running, tests should not be executed and failed.

That's when assumptions comes into picture.

org.junit.Assume class provides below methods to check assumptions.

1. assumeTrue
2. assumeFalse
3. assumeNotNull
4. assumeThat
5. assumeNoException

In below example, since assumption fails, test is ignored. Notice that test does not fail but ignored.

```java
package assumptions;

import org.junit.Assume;
import org.junit.Test;

/**
 * Created by Sagar on 30-04-2016.
 */
public class AssumeTest
{

    @Test
```

```
    public void test1()
    {

Assume.assumeTrue(ServiceCheck.isServiceRunning());
        System.out.println("This test will be
executed only " +
                "when above assumption is true");
    }
}

class ServiceCheck
{
    public static boolean isServiceRunning()
    {
        //code here to check if service is running
or not
        //if service is running, true is returned
else false is returned.
        return false;
    }
}
```

Here is the output of above code.

org.junit.AssumptionViolatedException: got: , expected: is

19. JUnit and Hamcrest Matchers

Junit 4.8+ onwards provides one assertion method called as assertthat.

assertThat method takes hamcrest matchers as arguments.

Below class contains all static methods used along with assertThat

`org.hamcrest.CoreMatchers`

Important methods in CoreMatchers class are given below.

1. is
2. not
3. nullValue
4. notNullValue
5. sameInstance
6. containsString
7. allOf
8. anyOf
9. equalTo
10. hasItems

Below example shows how to use hamcrest matchers in JUnit tests.

```
package hamcrest;
import org.junit.Assert;
import org.junit.Ignore;
import org.junit.Test;
```

```java
import java.util.Arrays;
import java.util.List;
import static org.junit.Assert.assertThat;

import static org.hamcrest.CoreMatchers.*;

    public class TestHamcrest
{

        @Test
        public void hi()
        {

            TestHamcrest m1 = new TestHamcrest();
            TestHamcrest m2 = m1;
            TestHamcrest m3 = null;

            //is matcher
            Assert.assertThat(111,is(100+11));
            Assert.assertThat(111,is(not(100+12)));
            assertThat(new String[]{"junit",
"hamcrest"}, is(new String[]{"junit", "hamcrest"}));

            //verification of null values
            assertThat(m3, nullValue());
            assertThat(m2, notNullValue());

            //checking if both variables point to
same object
            assertThat(m1, sameInstance(m2));

            //String verifications
            assertThat("hamcrest",
containsString("ham"));

            //assertions with list
            List<Integer> list = Arrays.asList(5, 2,
4);

            assertThat(list, hasItems(2, 5));

            //all of - used to make multiple
assertions at a time
```

```
                assertThat(4.12,
is(allOf(notNullValue(), instanceOf(Double.class),
equalTo(4.12))));

                //any of - used to make multiple
assertions at a time
                assertThat(4.12,
is(anyOf(notNullValue(), instanceOf(String.class),
equalTo(4.11))));

                //equalTo
                assertThat("Junit",
is(equalTo("Junit")));

                //instanceOf
                assertThat("Junit",
is(instanceOf(String.class)));

                //any of - used to make multiple
assertions at a time
                assertThat(4.12,
is(anyOf(notNullValue(), instanceOf(String.class),
equalTo(4.11))));

        }
}
```

20. Running JUnit tests in parallel

We can run tests in parallel in Junit by 2 ways.

1. using org.junit.experimental.ParallelComputer class.
2. By configuring maven surefire plug-in

1. using org.junit.experimental.ParallelComputer

Below example explains how to run multiple classes and methods in Parallel.

```
package parallel;

import org.junit.Test;
import org.junit.experimental.ParallelComputer;
import org.junit.runner.JUnitCore;

/**
 * Created by Sagar on 24-04-2016.
 */
public class ParallelTests
{

    @Test
    public void test()
    {
        Class[] testClasses =
{ParallelTestClassA.class,ParallelTestClassB.class
};

        System.out.println("running multiple classes
serially");

JUnitCore.runClasses(ParallelComputer.serial(),
testClasses);
```

```java
        System.out.println("running multiple classes
in parallel");

JUnitCore.runClasses(ParallelComputer.classes(),
testClasses);

        System.out.println("running methods in a
class in parallel");

JUnitCore.runClasses(ParallelComputer.methods(),
testClasses);

        System.out.println("running methods as well
classes in parallel");
        JUnitCore.runClasses(new
ParallelComputer(true, true), testClasses);
    }

    public static class ParallelTestClassA
    {
        @Test
        public void testA1()
        {
            System.out.println("Running A1");
        }

        @Test
        public void testA2(){
            System.out.println("Running A2");
        }
    }

    public static class ParallelTestClassB
{
        @Test public void testB1()
        {
            System.out.println("Running B1");
        }

        @Test public void testB2()
        {
            System.out.println("Running B2");
        }
    }
```

```
}
```

Here is the output of above example.

running multiple classes serially
Running A1
Running A2
Running B1
Running B2
running multiple classes in parallel
Running B1
Running B2
Running A1
Running A2
running methods in a class in parallel
Running A1
Running A2
Running B1
Running B2
methods as well classes in parallel
Running B2
Running B1
Running A1
Running A2

2. using Maven surefire plug-in

We can configure surefire plugin as shown below to run
tests in parallel. In below configuration, 10 threads will be
created at the same time - 1 for each test method.

<parallel> tag can take various values like classes, suites, both, all etc.

```
<configuration>

<includes><include>%regex[.*]</include></includes>

    <parallel>methods</parallel>

    <threadCount>10</threadCount>

</configuration>
```

Forked Execution

In forked execution, multiple JVMs are launched to execute the tests in separate processes.

21. Running JUnit tests with Maven

Note - I am using Maven Surefire plug-in version 2.19.1 and JUnit version 4.12. Ensure that you also use these versions or latest ones if available. Otherwise some commands may not work.

```
<dependency>

    <groupId>junit</groupId>

    <artifactId>junit</artifactId>

    <version>4.12</version>

    <scope>test</scope>

</dependency>
```

JUnit integrates very well with Maven. We can execute JUnit tests using Maven by various ways. In this post, we will see below topics.

1. Running all JUnit tests in a project using maven
2. Running JUnit tests from a specific test class (using maven command and through surefire plug-in configuration)
3. Running JUnit tests from specific categories (using maven command and through surefire plug-in configuration)
4. Surefire plug-in configuration for running JUnit tests

1. Running all JUnit tests

Simplest way to run all JUnit tests from your project is below command. To execute all tests, you will have to ensure that class names follow standard convention.

mvn test

2. Running tests from specific JUnit test classes

If you want to run tests from specific class, you can execute below command. In below example abc is the package and SanityTests is the name of Test class.

```
mvn test -Dtest=abc/SanityTests
```

In below example, all tests from 2 classes (validations/ValidationTests and junittests/FrontEndTests) will be executed.

```
mvn test -
Dtest=validations/ValidationTests,junittests/FrontEn
dTests
```

In below example, tests from all classes with their names ending with TestClass will be executed.

```
mvn test -Dtest=**/*TestClass
```

We can also configure test classes to be run through Maven surefire plug-in as mentioned below.

To run tests from all classes, you should use below surefire configuration.

```
<includes>

    <include>%regex[.*]</include>

</includes>
```

To run tests from specific classes, you should use below surefire configuration.

```
<includes>

<include>junittests.FrontEndTests,junittests.BackEnd
Tests</include>

</includes>
```

To exclude some tests from specific classes, you should use below surefire configuration.

```
<includes>

    <include>%regex[.*]</include>

</includes>

<excludes>

<exclude>junittests.FrontEndTests,junittests.BackEnd
Tests</exclude>

</excludes>
```

You can also use maven command as shown below to run tests from all classes except specific ones. Below command will run tests from

```
mvn test -Dtest=!validations.ValidationTests,**/*
```

3. Running specific test methods in Test class

We can also run only specific test methods in a test class. In below example, only 2 tests will run from ValidationTests class - test1 and test2

```
mvn test -
Dtest=validations/ValidationTests#test2+test1
```

In below example, all tests with name starting with test will be run from ValidationTests class.

```
mvn test -Dtest=validations/ValidationTests#test*
```

4. Running JUnit tests from specific categories

You can execute tests from specific categories by using groups switch. Below command will execute all tests belonging to mycategories.SanityTests category. Please ensure that surefire plug-in is configured properly as depicted below. Notice that we have included all classes in includes.

```
<groupId>org.apache.maven.plugins</groupId>

<artifactId>maven-surefire-plugin</artifactId>

<version>2.19.1</version>
```

```
<configuration>

    <includes>

        <include>%regex[.*]</include>

    </includes>

</configuration>

mvn test -Dgroups=mycategories.SanityTests
```

We can also run tests from multiple categories by using below command.

```
mvn test -
Dgroups=mycategories.SanityTests,mycategories.Regres
sionTests
```

Instead of command line, you can also run the tests from specific category by configuring the surefire plug-in as specified below. For example, in below configuration, we have specified that tests from SanityTests and RegressionTests categories should be executed.

```
<plugin>

  <groupId>org.apache.maven.plugins</groupId>

  <artifactId>maven-surefire-plugin</artifactId>

  <version>2.19.1</version>

  <configuration>

      <includes>
```

```
            <include>%regex[.*]</include>

        </includes>


    <groups>mycategories.SanityTests,mycategories.Regres
    sionTests</groups>

      </configuration>

    </plugin>
```

Sometimes, you might need to run tests from all groups except few ones. In that case, you can use below configuration. Notice ! in front of the category name. ! tells surefire plugin to select tests from all groups except mycategories.SanityTests

```
<configuration>

    <includes>

        <include>%regex[.*]</include>

    </includes>

    <groups>!mycategories.SanityTests</groups>

</configuration>
```

You can also execute the same command from command line as mentioned below.

```
mvn test -Dgroups=!mycategories.SanityTests
```

Alternatively, we can use excludedgroups tag.

```
<configuration>

<includes><include>%regex[.*]</include></includes>

<excludedGroups>mycategories.SanityTests</excludedGr
oups>

</configuration>
```

5. More Surefire plugin configuration for running JUnit tests

In this section, let us look at few more configurations of Surefire plug-in.

1. Skipping tests
2. Running tests in parallel
3. Using custom listener and reporter
4. Working with multiple modules

Skipping tests

Sometimes, we may need to skip the tests. In that scenario, you can use below command.

```
mvn test -DskipTests=true
```

Or you can skip the tests by configuring the surefire plug-in as well as shown below.

```
<configuration>

    <skipTests>true</skipTests>
```

```
</configuration>
```

22. JUnit and Gradle Integration

If you use a gradle as a build management tool, JUnit can be used to run the tests in your project.

JUnit configuration in build.gradle file

To use JUnit in your gradle project, you will have to configure your build.gradle file as shown below.

Key things to note about gradle build file are given below.

1. includeTestsMatching - This is used to specify the pattern for the test method and class names. To run all tests, you can use *.* pattern
2. includeCategories - This is used to include tests from specific category
3. excludeCategories - This is used to exclude tests from specific category

```
group 'org.softpost'
version '1.0-SNAPSHOT'

apply plugin: 'java'

repositories
{
    mavenCentral()
}

dependencies
{
    testCompile group: 'junit', name: 'junit',
version: '4.12'
}

test
```

```
{
    maxParallelForks=3
    useJUnit {
      //includeCategories '*.*'
      excludeCategories 'categories.CategoryY'
    }

    filter
    {
        //include specific method in any of the
tests
        includeTestsMatching "*.*"
    }
}
```

Running JUnit tests from command line

Below command is used to run all JUnit tests from the project.

gradle test

Below command is used to run all JUnit tests from the test classes SanityTests and SimpleTest.

test --tests categories.SanityTests --tests junit.SimpleTest

Below command is used to run specific JUnit test methods.
test --tests categories.SanityTests.testSanity1

Below command is used to run tests from classes with their names ending with SanityTests.

gradle test --tests *SanityTests

23. JUnit in Intellij IDEA

In this post, I am going tell you how to write JUnit tests in Intellij IDEA.

IntelliJ IDEA provides an excellent support to JUnit tests. JUnit plug-in is by default installed in IntelliJ IDEA.

Writing and executing JUnit tests is very simple in IntelliJ IDEA. You need to create a simple maven or gradle project and add JUnit dependency.

Adding JUnit dependency

If you are using Maven project, use below dependency in POM file.

```
<dependency>

    <groupId>junit</groupId>

    <artifactId>junit</artifactId>

    <version>4.12</version>

    <scope>test</scope>

</dependency>
```

If you are using Gradle project, add below lines in build.gradle file.

```
apply plugin: 'java'
```

```
dependencies {

testCompile 'junit:junit:4.12'

}
```

Writing JUnit Tests

We have already seen how to write simple JUnit tests.

Executing JUnit Tests in IntelliJ IDEA

We can execute JUnit tests in Intellij IDEA by right clicking on a test class and then selecting Run option as shown in below image.

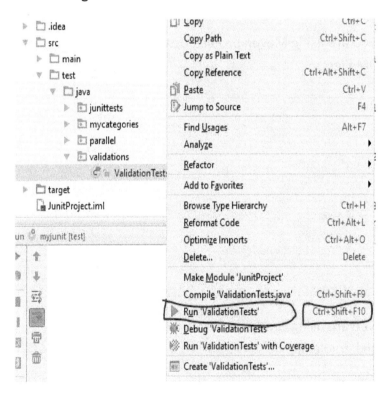

Running JUnit tests in IntelliJ IDEA

You can also use Ctrl+Shift+F10 shortcut key to run current JUnit test. To run Junit tests in specific package, you can right click on that package and click on run. Similarly to run all tests in all packages, you can right click on Java directory and click on Run all tests.

Viewing the JUnit test reports in IntelliJ IDEA

After running the JUnit tests, IntelliJ IDEA creates a beautiful HTML report. Below images show how to view JUnit HTML report generated by IntelliJ IDEA.

Below image shows sample output of Junit test execution. To export the report in HTML format, click on icon highlighted in yellow color.

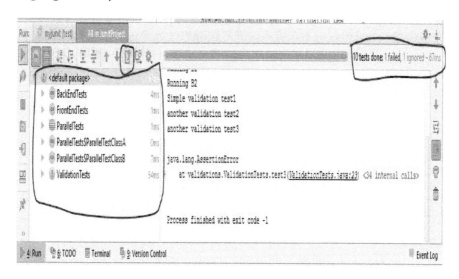

Export JUnit test execution report in IntelliJ IDEA

Below image shows sample JUnit test execution report generated by Intellij IDEA.

All in JunitProject: 67 ms
10 total, 1 failed, 1 ignored, 8 passed

Collapse | Expand

ParallelTests.test	ignored	1 ms
ParallelTests$ParallelTestClassA		0 ms
ParallelTests$ParallelTestClassA.testA1	passed	0 ms
Running A1		
ParallelTests$ParallelTestClassA.testA2	passed	0 ms
Running A2		
ParallelTests$ParallelTestClassB		7 ms
ParallelTests$ParallelTestClassB.testB1	passed	7 ms
Running B1		
ParallelTests$ParallelTestClassB.testB2	passed	0 ms
Running B2		
Validation Tests		54 ms

Sample JUnit test report generated by IntelliJ IDEA

If you are using a maven project, you can also execute JUnit tests using **maven commands.**

85

24. JUnit in Eclipse

In this post, let us learn how to write and execute JUnit tests in Eclipse.

Eclipse provides an excellent support to JUnit tests. Writing and executing JUnit tests is very simple in Eclipse. You need to create a simple maven or gradle project and add JUnit dependency.

Adding JUnit dependency

If you are using Maven project, use below dependency in POM file.

```
<dependency>

    <groupId>junit</groupId>

    <artifactId>junit</artifactId>

    <version>4.12</version>

    <scope>test</scope>

</dependency>
```

If you are using Gradle project, add below lines in build.gradle file.

```
apply plugin: 'java'

 dependencies {
```

```
testCompile 'junit:junit:4.12'

}
```

Writing JUnit Tests

We have already seen how to write simple JUnit tests.

Executing JUnit Tests in Eclipse

We can execute JUnit tests in Eclipse by right clicking on a test class and then selecting Run as JUnit option as shown in below image.

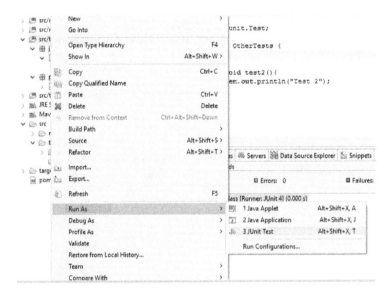

Running JUnit tests in Eclipse

You can also use Alt+Shift+X, T shortcut key to run current JUnit test. To run Junit tests in specific package, you can right click on that package and click on Run as Junit Test. Similarly to run all tests in all packages, you can right click on Java directory and click on Run all tests as JUnit Test.

Viewing the JUnit test reports in Eclipse

After running the JUnit tests, JUnit runner creates a simple xml report. Below images show how to view JUnit report generated by JUnit runner in Eclipse.

JUnit reports in Eclipse

If you are using a maven project, you can also execute JUnit tests using **maven commands**.